# Super Snack Time

# Recipes

Your #1 Cookbook of Quick Healthy
Munchies!

# Table of Contents

# Introduction

Why would you take the time to make homemade snacks, instead of just grabbing some at the grocery when you do your routine shopping?

Most parents would agree that worrying about what their families eat can be a big responsibility. Feeding your children healthy snacks is an excellent way to set them up to make good food choices as they grow. It's important to provide your family with healthy, quality snacks, not just more calories.

These snack recipes are wonderful for kids and adults alike! You'll like taking healthier snacks to work during the week and having healthy things to snack on at home with your kids. You may be looking for snacks to eat on the go, or munchies to keep in the house. This cookbook offers treats that everyone will love!

Making good choices in snacks is difficult - very difficult. But if you use this cookbook and your own creativity, you can create healthy snacks

Whether you're looking for quick snacks to grab and go, or things to stock your fridge with, so the kids will have something to snack on, instead of eating junk food, try these recipes today!

# 1 – Pita Cups

These are SO easy to make! With hummus, cheese and healthy veggies, this recipe will give you a chance to utilize your muffin tins more. They can help you make this totally easy snack.

**Makes** 9 Servings

**Cooking + Prep Time:** 35 minutes

**Ingredients:**

- 3 pita breads
- 1 x 17-ounce container of hummus, garlic
- 2 tbsp. of oil, olive
- 1/2 cup of cucumber, diced
- 1/4 cup of Kalamata olives, pitted, chopped
- 2 tsp. of parsley, chopped
- 2 tsp. of dill, chopped
- 3 oz. of feta cheese crumbles
- 9 halved tomatoes, grape or cherry

**Instructions:**

1. Preheat the oven to 350F. Spritz the muffin tin cups with nonstick spray. Slice pitas into six slices each. Place the triangles in muffin cups. Press them down gently so they form bowls.

2. Bake pitas for five to seven minutes, till light gold in color. Allow to cool for eight to 10 minutes. Remove pita bowls. Fill them halfway with the hummus.

3. Combine dill, parsley, olives, cucumbers and oil in large sized bowl. Top hummus cups with spoons full of cucumber mixture.

4. Top cups with sprinkling of feta cheese and 1/2 grape or cherry tomato. Serve.

# 2 – Baked Brie and Cranberry Cups

Baked Brie is becoming even more popular lately. It **Makes** great snacks and appetizers. In this recipe, the Brie is complemented with cranberry sauce and baked into individual-sized tarts, with a pre-made crust to make it easy.

**Makes** 24 Bites

**Cooking + Prep Time:** 40 minutes

**Ingredients:**

- 1 x 7-8 oz. pie crust, prepared
- 1/2 cup of cranberry sauce, canned
- 3 oz. of cubed Brie cheese, 24 cubes

- Optional: 1 tbsp. of chopped chives, fresh

**Instructions:**

1. Preheat the oven to 450F. Coat mini muffin tin lightly with non-stick spray.

2. Unroll the prepared pie crust onto work surface. Flatten the dough to 12" diameter. Cut 24 x 2" circles from dough. Reroll the scraps and use that dough too, if needed.

3. Place dough circles into muffin cups. Press gently on sides and bottoms. Prick dough with fork.

4. Bake till browned lightly. This usually takes five to seven minutes. Remove pan from oven.

5. Add 1 tsp. of cranberry sauce to cups. Top them with Brie cubes. Return to oven. Bake till cheese is melted and sauce has become hot. Allow to cool for eight to 10 minutes. Sprinkle cups with chives, as desired. Serve cups warm.

# 3 – Jicama Snacks

Not only is this a crunchy snack, but it also has super flavor and it's healthy, too. Your kids will love it, and they can even help you make it if you like.

**Makes** 6 Servings

**Cooking + Prep Time:** 12 minutes

**Ingredients:**

- 1 jicama, large
- 2 fresh limes, juice only
- Red pepper, crushed, as desired

**Instructions:**

1. Peel the jicama. Cut into sticks the shape of French fries.

2. Combine with lime juice and red pepper, if desired, in medium sized bowl. Toss and coat well. Serve.

# 4 – Broccoli Cheese Bread

This is a filling appetizer or snack that doesn't take long and tastes great. If you wring out the steamed broccoli with cheese cloth or paper towels, it will ensure that your finished cheesy bread is crisp and not soggy.

**Makes** 8 Servings

**Cooking + Prep Time:** 45 minutes

**Ingredients:**

- 3 cups of broccoli, riced
- 1 egg, large
- 1 1/2 cup of mozzarella shreds
- 1/4 cup of Parmesan cheese, grated

- 2 minced garlic cloves
- 1/2 tsp. of oregano, dried
- Salt, kosher
- Pepper, black ground
- Optional: a pinch of red pepper flakes, crushed, if desired
- 2 tsp. of fresh parsley, chopped
- To serve: warmed marinara sauce

**Instructions:**

1. Preheat the oven to 425F. Line large-sized cookie sheet with baking paper.

2. Microwave the riced broccoli for one minute. Wring out excess moisture with cheese cloth or paper towels.

3. Transfer the broccoli to large sized bowl. Add garlic, Parmesan, 1 cup of mozzarella and egg. Season as desired.

4. Transfer this dough to a cookie sheet. Shape it into a round, thin crust.

5. Bake till dried out and golden, usually 15 to 20 minutes. Then top with the last 1/2 cup of mozzarella cheese. Bake till crust becomes crispy and cheese has melted.

6. Garnish as desired. Serve cheese bread with the warmed marinara sauce.

# 5 – Turkey and Spinach Roll-ups

Use a bit of nutmeg, along with sweet pepper strips and honey mustard, to jazz up these tasty turkey wraps. They're delicious and healthy, too!

**Makes** 8 Servings

**Cooking + Prep Time:** 25 minutes

## Ingredients:

- 2 tsp. of mustard, honey
- 1 dash of nutmeg, ground
- 8 thin slices of turkey breast, smoked or oven-roasted - pre-packaged deli turkey is fine
- 1 cup of basil leaves, fresh
- 1/2 med. sized de-seeded, strip-sliced sweet pepper, green or red
- 4 lengthways cut sticks of string cheese, low fat
- Optional: basil leaves or sprigs, fresh, small

## Instructions:

1. Stir nutmeg and honey mustard together in small sized bowl. Spread mixture carefully on slices of turkey.

2. Divide basil leaves over slices of turkey. Place them on short edges of slices. Allow the tips of the leaves to extend a bit beyond edge of turkey slices. Top with cheese and pepper strips.

3. Start at edges with vegetables and cheese and roll up they turkey slices. Garnish as desired. Slice rolls in halves and serve.

# 6 – Chicken Won Tons

Do you often have some leftover chicken in the fridge? This snack gives you an easy way to use it up. It **Makes** a great snack for guests who drop by unexpectedly, and it's a healthy alternative to junk food. Even the little ones love these snacks.

**Makes** 12 Servings

**Cooking + Prep Time:** 50 minutes

**Ingredients:**

- 1 x 14-oz. pkg. of wonton wrappers
- 1 lb. of chicken, shredded and cooked

**Instructions:**

1. Preheat the oven to 350F.

2. Place a little shredded chicken lengthways on won ton wrappers. Roll them up. Dampen edges of wrappers with water to seal.

3. Once your chicken has run out, place the rolled won tons on greased 13x9" baking dish.

4. Bake won tons at 350F for 14-20 minutes, till wrappers are crisp, then cool a bit and serve.

# 7 – Spice and Latte Pumpkin Snacks

These pumpkin snacks are actually inspired by Starbucks™ pumpkin spiced latte. They include the great tastes of coffee, pumpkin and other spices, and they give you extra protein to help you get through your busy day.

**Makes** 30 snacks

**Cooking + Prep Time:** 45 minutes

## Ingredients:

- 3 scoops of protein powder, vanilla bean
- 1/2 cup of oats, instant
- 1 1/2 tsp. of cinnamon, ground
- 1/4 tsp. of ginger, ground
- 1/8 tsp. of nutmeg, ground
- 1 cup of pureed pumpkin – don't use a pumpkin pie mix
- 1 1/2 tsp. of coffee granules, instant
- 1/2 tsp. of Stevia®, vanilla crème, +/- as desired

## Instructions:

1. Line cookie sheet with baking paper.

2. Combine ginger, nutmeg, cinnamon, oats and protein powder in medium sized bowl.

3. In separate bowl, stir Stevia®, pumpkin puree and instant coffee together till coffee fully dissolves. Add oat mixture in this bowl. Mix till all ingredients are incorporated well.

4. Divide mixture into 30 same-size portions. Roll portions into small spheres. Place them on prepared cookie sheet. Refrigerate and serve when chilled.

# 8 – Peanut Butter Poppers

This is a sweet-tasting snack that brings peanut butter to a new level. It works especially well at children's parties or play dates. You'll top the mini, sweet rice cakes with a blend of cream cheese and peanut butter, along with sugar-free preserves.

**Makes** 4 Servings

**Cooking + Prep Time:** 20 minutes

**Ingredients:**

- 1/3 cup of softened cream cheese spread, light
- 1 tbsp. of peanut butter, powdered
- 1/4 tsp. of apple pie or ground ginger spice

- 12 mini rice cakes, apple cinnamon or caramel corn
- 1/4 cup of preserves, sugar free, your choice of flavor

**Instructions:**

1. Stir ginger, cream cheese and peanut butter together in small sized bowl.

2. Evenly spread on the rice cakes and top with your favorite preserves. Serve.

# 9 – Spiced Crunchy Chick Peas

This snack, I should warn you, is very addictive. If you just make one batch each time, it will be better, because even if you make a double batch, they will still disappear quickly. You can use any spice combinations you enjoy to season the chick peas.

**Makes** 4 Servings

**Cooking + Prep Time:** 1 hour 15 minutes + 24 hours of soaking time

**Ingredients:**

- 1 cup of chick peas
- 2 tbsp. of oil, olive
- A pinch each of cumin, paprika and cayenne pepper, as desired
- Salt, kosher, as desired
- Pepper, ground black, as desired

**Instructions:**

1. Place the chick peas in large sized container. Cover with a few inches of cool, filtered water and allow to set for about 24 hours. Drain them and dry them on top of paper towels.

2. Preheat the oven to 400F.

3. Pour the chick peas in baking dish. Drizzle oil over top. Season as desired. Coat chick peas by stirring.

4. Bake in 400F oven. Stir every 15-20 minutes or so until they are fragrant and crispy. This usually takes about an hour. Transfer chick peas to wire rack for additional cooling. Serve.

# 10 – Zucchini Sushi

Zucchini sushi may remind you a bit of spicy California rolls, except that they don't include any rice. These are fresher, though, plus easier to put together, and healthier for you.

**Makes** 2 Servings

**Cooking + Prep Time:** 25 minutes

**Ingredients:**

- 2 zucchinis, medium
- 4 ounces of softened cream cheese
- 1 tsp. of sriracha sauce
- 1 tsp. of lime juice, fresh

- 1 cup of crab meat, lump
- 1/2 matchstick-sliced carrot
- 1/2 diced avocado
- 1/2 matchstick-sliced cucumber
- 1 tsp. of sesame seeds, toasted

**Instructions:**

1. Slice zucchinis into flat, thin strips with veggie peeler. Place them on a plate lined with paper towels, to drain.

2. Combine lime juice, cream cheese and sriracha in medium sized bowl.

3. Lay slices of zucchini down on cutting board. Spread cream cheese on top thinly. Top left side with 1 pinch each cucumber, avocados, carrots and crab meat.

4. Start from left side and roll zucchini slices tightly. Sprinkle with toasted sesame seeds and serve.

# 11 – Watermelon Salsa

The crunchy, sweet and savory salsa in this snack is a great accompaniment for grilled chicken or pork. You can also serve it with plain tortilla chips, instead of using tomato salsa.

**Makes** 8 Servings

**Cooking + Prep Time:** 25 minutes

**Ingredients:**

- 3 cups of diced watermelon, seedless
- 2 de-seeded, minced jalapeno peppers, as desired
- 1/3 cup of cilantro, chopped

- 1/4 cup of lime juice, fresh
- 1/4 cup of minced onion, red
- 1/4 tsp. of salt, kosher, as desired

**Instructions:**

1. Place onion, lime juice, cilantro, jalapenos and watermelon in medium sized bowl. Combine well by stirring. Season with kosher salt. Serve after making, or chill and serve.

# 12 – Sriracha and Lemon Kale Chips

You won't be able to pretend you're munching on potato chips when you eat kale chips, but if you're on the fence about kale, these chips may win you over with their tastiness.

**Makes** 2 Servings

**Cooking + Prep Time:** 45 minutes

**Ingredients:**

- 1 bunch of kale, medium in size
- 2 tbsp. of oil, olive

- 1 tbsp. of sriracha sauce
- 2 tsp. of lime juice, fresh
- 1/4 tsp. of salt, kosher

**Instructions:**

1. Preheat the oven to 300F. Line two cookie sheets with parchment paper.

2. Wash the kale well. Remove ribs and discard them. Dry the leaves well. You can use a salad spinner if you have one. Be sure there is no moisture remaining. Tear the leaves of kale into pieces of two or three inches each.

3. Blend the lime juice, salt, sriracha sauce and oil together in large bowl, using a whisk. Add the kale and toss well to coat it.

4. Divide the kale on your prepped cookie sheets. Be sure they don't overlap.

5. Bake in 300F oven for 12-15 minutes. Flip pieces that appear too brown. Continue to bake till kale becomes crisp. This usually takes 10-15 more minutes.

6. Allow the kale chips to cool for three to five minutes. Serve.

# 13 – Poppy Seed Lemon Bites

These yummy bites taste like classic muffins, but they are way easier to make up, and lower in calories, too. You can store leftovers for up to six days in the fridge.

**Makes** 28 bites

**Cooking + Prep Time:** 25 minutes

## Ingredients:

- 1/2 cup of oats, old-fashioned
- 1 tbsp. of poppy seeds
- 3 scoops of protein powder, vanilla
- 1/2 tbsp. of Truvia sweetener
- 1 tsp. of lemon zest, freshly grated
- 6 tbsp. of lemon juice, fresh squeezed
- 6 tbsp. of water, filtered

## Instructions:

1. Combine lemon zest, Truvia®, poppy seeds, oats and protein powder in large sized bowl. Add water and lemon juice and stir till incorporated fully.

2. Shape mixture into 28 small sized balls. Place in airtight container. Keep in fridge till you serve.

# 14 – Spiced Energy Trail Mix

This delicious trail mix is made with sweet dates and mangos, and pumpkin seeds. The spice rub gives it a nice dose of heat.

**Makes** 2 Servings

**Cooking + Prep Time:** 10 minutes

**Ingredients:**

- 2 oz. of pumpkin seeds
- 3 oz. of mango, dried
- 2 oz. of dates, chopped, pitted

- 1/2 tsp. of spice rub, store-bought

**Instructions:**

1. Combine the pumpkin seeds, mango and dates with the spice rub. Serve.

# 15 – Cinnamon Potato Chips

You don't have to wolf down potato chips to fill that hunger for a salty snack. These cinnamon potato chips have the taste of crunchy, crisp, thin slices of cinnamon toast. Yum!

**Makes** 4 Servings

**Cooking + Prep Time:** 40 minutes

## Ingredients:

- 2 peeled, sliced sweet potatoes
- 1 tbsp. of butter, melted
- 1/2 tsp. of salt, kosher
- 2 tsp. of sugar, brown
- 1/2 tsp. of cinnamon, ground

## Instructions:

1. Preheat the oven to 400F. Spray two baking sheets with non-stick spray.

2. Arrange the sweet potato slices in one layer on two baking sheets.

3. Stir cinnamon, brown sugar, salt and butter together in small sized bowl. Brush it onto the sliced sweet potatoes.

4. Bake in 400F oven till edges begin curling upwards. This usually takes 18-25 minutes. Remove from oven and allow to cool just a bit. Serve.

# 16 – Quinoa Bagel Crackers

These may well become your favorite snack crackers! They have the crunch you love, with the best seasonings. Feel free to make a double batch, or you won't have any leftovers to munch on tomorrow.

**Makes** 5 Servings

**Cooking + Prep Time:** 1 1/4 hours

**Ingredients:**

- 1 cup of quinoa flour, + extra to roll dough in
- 2 tsp. of "Everything but the Bagel" or similar store-bought seasoning mix
- 5 1/2 tbsp. of warm water, filtered
- 1 tsp. of oil, olive
- 1/4 tsp. of salt, kosher

**Instructions:**

1. Preheat oven to 350F.

2. Whisk seasoning and quinoa flour in medium sized bowl.

3. Make an indentation in the middle. Pour in oil and water. Mix ingredients all together, forming dough.

4. Flour your rolling pin and work surface mat with flour. Transfer dough to mat. Roll dough out to about 1/16-inch thickness.

5. Slice dough into 1-inch squares. Separate them as much as you can, so they will bake more evenly. Sprinkle salt over the top and pat it gently into dough.

6. Slide mat onto baking sheet. Bake in preheated oven for 20-30 minutes, till crackers are crunchy and golden.

7. Cool crackers well on baking sheet and transfer to airtight container or serve.

# 17 – Cheese 'n Pimento Snack Spread

This is a Southern snacking favorite with a simple blending of pimentos, cheddar cheese and mayo. You can add some hot sauce if you like it spicy. Serve it with crackers if you like.

**Makes** 12 Servings

**Cooking + Prep Time:** 20 minutes

## Ingredients:

- 1 1/2 cups of cheddar cheese shreds, reduced fat
- 1/4 cup of mayo, low-fat
- 1 x 4-oz. jar of drained, chopped pimentos, sliced
- 2 tbsp. of scallions, minced
- Optional: hot sauce

## Instructions:

1. Combine the hot sauce, if desired, with scallions, pimentos, mayo and cheese in medium sized bowl. If there are any leftovers, you can cover them and keep in your fridge for three days.

# 18 – Apple Chips

These tasty apple chips will be gone as soon as you set them out for your family or guests. They are a great choice for healthy snacks, and they're easy to take with you to-go. Baking at a low temp for a longer time will dehydrate the apples more effectively and bring out their flavor.

**Makes** 6 Servings

**Cooking + Prep Time:** 1 hour 40 minutes

**Ingredients:**

- 2 cored sliced apples, Golden Delicious, if available
- 1 1/2 tsp. of sugar, white
- 1/2 tsp. of cinnamon, ground

**Instructions:**

1. Preheat the oven to 225F.

2. Arrange sliced apples on metal cookie sheet.

3. Mix cinnamon and sugar together in small sized bowl. Sprinkle it over the apples.

4. Bake at 225F till apples dry and curl their edges up. This usually takes between 45 minutes and an hour.

5. Transfer the apple chips to wire rack till cooled off and crispy. Serve.

# 19 – Coffee-Kissed Bliss Bites

These energy bites can be the perfect mid-morning snack, especially since they are kissed with coffee. The will keep for a week or so in the fridge in an airtight container.

**Makes** 30 bites

**Cooking + Prep Time:** 35 minutes

**Ingredients:**

- 3/4 cup of warm milk, non-fat
- 1 tbsp. of coffee granules, instant

- 1/2 tsp. of Stevia® vanilla cream flavor, as desired
- 3 scoops of protein powder, vanilla bean
- 1/2 cup of oats, instant

**Instructions:**

1. Add instant coffee and milk to medium sized bowl. Stir till coffee granules have dissolved completely. It is a bit time-consuming.

2. Add Stevia® and stir in. Pour in oats and protein powder. Stir till incorporated completely.

3. Line cookie sheet with baking paper.

4. Work with small amounts of mixture and shape into balls. Chill and serve. Transfer leftover balls to airtight container. Refrigerate when not serving.

# 20 – White Bean Hummus

This snack-worthy hummus features tahini nuttiness and a taste like peanut butter, but it's made with sesame seeds. The beans have lots of protein, so they're healthy, too.

**Makes** 1 1/4 cups

**Cooking + Prep Time:** 10 minutes

**Ingredients:**

- 2 peeled cloves of garlic
- 1 x 15-oz. can of rinsed, drained cannellini beans
- 1/4 cup of tahini

- 3 tbsp. of lemon juice, fresh
- 1 1/2 tsp. of cumin, ground
- 1/4 tsp. of salt, kosher
- 1/4 tsp. of red pepper flakes, crushed
- 2 tbsp. of minced parsley, fresh
- Wedge-cut pita breads
- Assorted veggies, fresh

**Instructions:**

1. Place the garlic cloves in food processor. Cover. Process till minced fully.

2. Add salt, cumin, pepper flakes, lemon juice, tahini and beans. Process till texture is smooth.

3. Transfer mixture to small sized bowl. Add parsley and combine. Refrigerate till you serve. Serve with assorted veggies and pita bread wedges.

# 21 – Fruit Fun Skewers

Snacks don't COME any easier than this one. Just prep your favorite fruits and slide them onto skewers. They're so fun that even kids will love eating their fruit.

**Makes** 5 Servings

**Cooking + Prep Time:** 20 minutes

**Ingredients:**

- 5 halved strawberries, large
- 1/4 cubed cantaloupe
- 2 peeled, chunk-cut bananas

- 1 chunk-cut apple
- 20 small skewers

**Instructions:**

1. Thread the apple, banana, cantaloupe and strawberry pieces alternately on skewers. Arrange fruit skewers in a decorative way on a serving platter. Serve.

# 22 – Coconut Chips

Coconut flakes are SO addictive, the whole family loves them. The cinnamon, nutmeg and allspice give them a special taste, and they are still salty, crunchy and delicious.

**Makes** 2 Servings

**Cooking + Prep Time:** 10 minutes

**Ingredients:**

- 1 cup of coconut flakes, unsweetened
- 1 tsp. of cinnamon, ground
- 1/4 tsp. each nutmeg and allspice
- 1/4 tsp. of salt, kosher

- 1 tsp. of melted oil, coconut

**Instructions:**

1. Preheat the oven to 350F. Line cookie sheet with baking paper.

2. Put coconut flakes in zipper top bag. Pour salt, allspice, nutmeg and cinnamon on top. Shake quickly.

3. Pour coconut oil into bag. Shake to coat the flakes completely.

4. Pour coated coconut on cookie sheet. Place in oven.

5. Bake for three to five minutes. Don't allow them to burn or over-brown.

6. Remove from the oven. Place on another pan to prevent any extra browning. Serve.

# 23 – Tamale Cakes

Are you tired of serving peanut butter and jelly for handy snacks? These tamale cakes have lots of flavor, and no fuss. Pair them up with the skewered fruit above, if you like.

**Makes** 2 dozen cakes

**Cooking + Prep Time:** 50 minutes

**Ingredients:**

- 2 x 8 1/2 oz. pkgs. of corn muffin/bread mix
- 1 x 14 3/4 oz. can of corn, cream style

- 2 eggs, large, beaten lightly
- 1 1/2 cups of Mexican cheese blend shreds, reduced fat
- 1 1/2 cups of chicken breast, chopped and cooked
- 3/4 cup of enchilada sauce, red

**Instructions:**

1. Preheat the oven to 400F.

2. Combine the muffin mix, eggs and corn. Stir till barely moistened. Add 1 cup of cheese shreds and stir. Toss chicken in another bowl with enchilada sauce.

3. Fill 24 foil-lined muffin tin cups with 2 tbsp. butter each. Place a tbsp. of the chicken mixture in middle of each one. Cover with 1 more tbsp. +/- of butter.

4. Bake till they are golden brown. Sprinkle the tops with the rest of the cheese. Bake till the cheese melts. Cool for five more minutes, then move to wire cooling racks. Serve warm.

# 24 – Sweet Monkey Brains

This cinnamon-y, gooey recipe is good enough to impress guests and the family, too. It is super easy to make and is a take-off from the traditional monkey brains.

**Makes** 6 Servings

**Cooking + Prep Time:** 35 minutes

## Ingredients:

- 3 x 7 1/2 oz. pkgs. of biscuit dough, refrigerated
- 1/3 cup of sugar, white
- 2 tsp. of cinnamon, ground
- 1/2 cup of pecans, chopped
- 1/2 cup of melted butter, unsalted
- 1/2 cup of sugar, brown

## Instructions:

1. Preheat oven to 350F. Lightly spray 6 mini Bundt pans.

2. Stir cinnamon and white sugar together in small sized bowl. Set it aside.

3. Use a knife or scissors to cut biscuits into various shapes and sizes.

4. Sprinkle half of pecans or so among six prepared pans. Roll the biscuit pieces in cinnamon and sugar mixture. Place them in pans, evenly.

5. Mix melted butter with brown sugar. Add remaining pecans and stir. Distribute the mixture evenly over dough ball pans.

6. Bake for 15-20 minutes at 350F. Biscuits should be cooked through and toasted.

7. Remove from oven. Invert individual Bundt pans onto plates while hot. Serve.

# 25 – Parsley Potato Chips

Could this be a healthier potato chip? It sure tastes like it! This is a quick recipe for making baked potato chips, which are so much healthier than bagged, fried chips. Be sure that you slice the potatoes evenly so they'll all cook well.

**Makes** 2-4 Servings

**Cooking + Prep Time:** 30 minutes

**Ingredients:**

- 2 sliced potatoes
- 1 tbsp. of oil, olive
- 1 tbsp. of chopped parsley

- Salt, sea, as desired

**Instructions:**

1. Preheat the oven to 425F.

2. Wash potatoes. Slice them thinly, width-ways. Lay in a single layer on cookie sheet. Toss with 1 tbsp. of oil, then sea salt and ground pepper.

3. Bake potatoes till crisp and golden brown. This takes 20 minutes or so. Toss with sea salt and chopped parsley. Serve.

# 26 – Oat Rhubarb Bars

These chewy, oat-filled rhubarb bars will give you the perfect mix of sweetness and tartness. They are hard to beat, for flavor and healthiness.

**Makes** 15 Servings

**Cooking + Prep Time:** 50 minutes

**Ingredients:**

- 1 1/2 cups of rhubarb, frozen or fresh
- 1 cup of sugar, brown, packed

- 4 tbsp. of water, filtered
- 1 tsp. of lemon juice, fresh
- 4 tsp. of corn starch
- 1 cup of oats, old-fashioned
- 3/4 cup of flour, all-purpose
- 1/2 cup of coconut, shredded, sweetened
- 1/2 tsp. of salt, kosher
- 1/3 cup of melted butter, unsalted

**Instructions:**

1. Combine rhubarb with lemon juice, 3 tbsp. of water and 1/2 cup of brown sugar in large sized sauce pan. Lower heat to med. Stir while cooking for four to five minutes, till the rhubarb becomes tender.

2. Combine remaining water and corn starch till mixture is smooth. Stir this gradually into the rhubarb mixture.

3. Bring to boil. Stir and cook for a couple minutes, till mixture thickens. Remove from heat and set it aside.

4. Combine remaining brown sugar with salt, coconut, flour and oats in large sized bowl. Add butter and stir well till you have a crumbly mixture.

5. Press 1/2 of oats mixture in an 8-inch greased baking dish. Spread with the rhubarb mixture. Sprinkle using remainder of the oat mixture. Lightly press down.

6. Bake for 25-30 minutes at 350F till golden brown in color. Cool on rack and cut the mixture into squares. Serve.

# 27 – Chocolate Chip Energy Bites

Here is an all-new take on no-bake cookies. They are so tasty and SO good for you, too! Be prepared to have people asking for your recipe when you serve them. They're a hit with adults and children alike.

**Makes** 24 Servings

**Cooking + Prep Time:** 1 hour 20 minutes

**Ingredients:**

- 1 cup of oats, rolled
- 1/2 cup of chocolate chips, semi-sweet, miniature

- 1/2 cup of flax seed, ground
- 1/2 cup of peanut butter, crunchy
- 1/3 cup of honey, organic
- 1 tsp. of vanilla extract, pure

**Instructions:**

1. Combine the vanilla extract, honey, peanut butter, flax seed, chocolate chips and oats together in medium bowl. Use your hands to form the mixture into balls.

2. Arrange snacks on cookie sheet. Freeze for an hour or so, till they set. Serve.

# 28 – Yogurt Covered Blueberries

This is a simple recipe, just dipping the blueberries in yogurt, placing them on foil and freezing them. Resist the temptation to eat some of the yogurt while you're preparing the snack, or the blueberries won't be as tasty.

**Makes** 2 Servings

**Cooking + Prep Time:** 5 minutes

**Ingredients:**

- 6 ounces of Greek yogurt, plain, non-fat
- 1 1/2 scoops of nutritional shake mix
- 1 cup of blueberries, frozen

**Instructions:**

1. Line 13x9" pan using foil.

2. Mix nutritional shake mix with yogurt in small sized bowl.

3. Toss in just a few blueberries and coat them with yogurt. Remove with three toothpicks.

4. Place on foil-lined pan.

5. Repeat till you have covered all the blueberries.

6. Freeze for an hour or so, till yogurt freezes.

7. Keep them frozen till ready to serve.

# 29 – Carrot Cookies

This snack recipe has been in many families for a long time. The cookies are delicious and soft, and when you get a whiff of them cooking, it's hard to resist them.

**Makes** 7 dozen cookies

**Cooking + Prep Time:** 1/2 hour

**Ingredients:**

- 2/3 cup of shortening
- 1 cup of sugar, brown, packed

- 2 eggs, large
- 1/2 cup of butter milk
- 1 tsp. of vanilla extract, pure
- 2 cups of flour, all-purpose
- 1 tsp. of cinnamon, ground
- 1/2 tsp, of salt, sea
- 1/4 tsp. of baking soda
- 1/4 tsp. of baking powder
- 1/4 tsp. of nutmeg, ground
- 1/4 tsp. of cloves, ground
- 2 cups of oats, quick-cooking
- 1 cup of carrots, shredded
- 1/2 cup of pecans, chopped

**Instructions:**

1. Cream the brown sugar and shortening in large sized bowl till fluffy and light. Beat vanilla, eggs and butter milk in.

2. Combine cloves, nutmeg, baking soda, baking powder, salt, cinnamon and flour together. Add gradually to the creamed mixture. Add pecans, oats and carrots and stir well.

3. Drop the dough in rounded teaspoons on ungreased cookie sheets, with a couple inches between them. Bake them at

375F till they brown lightly. This usually takes between six and eight minutes or so. Remove the snacks to rack for cooling. Serve.

# 30 – Zucchini Chips

Zucchini is a versatile ingredient, since you can do so much with it. It can be spiralized for stir fries or shredded and included in dishes like meatballs. In this recipe, you'll be introduced to zucchini chips, and they are SO tasty.

**Makes** 4 Servings

**Cooking + Prep Time:** 20 minutes

**Ingredients:**

- 2 zucchinis, medium, sliced at 1/4" thickness
- 1/2 cup of bread crumbs, dry, seasoned
- 1/8 tsp. of pepper, black, ground

- 2 tbsp. of Parmesan cheese, grated
- 2 whites from large eggs

**Instructions:**

1. Preheat oven to 475F.

2. Stir Parmesan cheese, pepper and bread crumbs together in a small sized bowl.

3. In separate bowl, place egg whites.

4. Dip the slices of zucchini into egg white bowl, then coat with bread crumb mixture. Place on greased cookie sheet.

5. Bake at 475F for four to six minutes. Turn them over and bake for five to 10 minutes longer, till they are crispy and brown. Serve.

# 31 – Berry Oat Treats

These delicious treats are easy to make, and they are a substantial and filling alternative to conventional granola bars.

**Makes** 12 Servings

**Cooking + Prep Time:** 50 minutes

**Ingredients:**

- 1/2 cup softened butter, unsalted
- 1/2 cup sugar, brown, packed

- 1 egg, large
- 1 banana, ripe but not over-ripe
- 3 personal size tubes Go-Gurt yogurt, flavor of your choice
- 2 1/2 cups of oats
- 1/2 cup strawberries, diced
- Optional: 1/2 cup walnuts, chopped

**Instructions:**

1. Heat the oven to 350F. Place paper cups in 12 muffin cups.

2. Beat sugar and butter in large sized bowl with med-speed electric mixer, till fluffy and light.

3. Add banana and egg. Beat till mixed well. Beat in the yogurt. Add and stir walnuts, oats and dried strawberries. Evenly divide this mixture in muffin cups.

4. Bake for 25 minutes, till tops are a golden brown. Cool on a rack for 10-15 minutes and serve.

# 32 – Pizza Snacks

This is a new and easy twist on a conventional pizza roll. The fresh basil and prosciutto make it unique and tasty.

**Makes** 16 Servings

**Cooking + Prep Time:** 40 minutes

**Ingredients:**

- Non-stick spray
- 1 x 8-ounce can of tomato sauce
- 1 x 6-ounce can of tomato paste
- 1 tsp. of vinegar, white, distilled

- 1 tsp. of basil, dried
- 1 tsp. of garlic powder
- 1/8 tsp. of pepper, black, ground
- 2 tsp. of oregano, dried
- 2 tbsp. of oil, olive
- 1 x 16-ounce package of pizza dough, ready to bake
- 3 oz. of prosciutto
- 1 cup of mozzarella cheese shreds, part-skim
- 1 cup of basil, fresh, chopped

**Instructions:**

1. Preheat the oven to 425F. Spray cookie sheet with non-stick spray.

2. Mix 2 tsp. oil, 1 tsp. of oregano, garlic, basil, vinegar, tomato paste and tomato sauce together in small sized bowl. This is your pizza sauce.

3. Roll out the dough into 8 1/2 x 14" rectangle. Spread 1/2 cup of pizza sauce from step 2 over dough evenly. Reserve some for dipping.

4. Lay prosciutto out on the top. Sprinkle with basil and cheese.

5. Cut dough lengthways in half with a pizza cutter. Cut both halves into eight strips. Roll the strips and place with seam side facing down on cookie sheet.

6. Brush the tops of pizza rolls with the rest of the oil. Sprinkle with the rest of the oregano. Bake for 10-12 minutes, till golden brown. Remove from oven and allow to cool a bit. Serve.

# 33 – Walnut Fig Mini Cheese Balls

These tasty cheese balls use some ingredients you likely have in your pantry or fridge right now. They will absolutely be the stars of your next dinner party.

**Makes** 8 Servings

**Cooking + Prep Time:** 20 minutes

**Ingredients:**

- 4 ounces of goat cheese, creamy
- 4 ounces of cream cheese, softened
- 1/4 cup of fig jam
- 1 cup of walnuts, chopped

**Instructions:**

1. Stir the jam, goat cheese and cream cheese in a medium sized bowl till blended well.

2. Shape the mixture into balls of about one inch each. Roll in the walnuts and coat them. It's okay if some cheese shows through.

3. Place mini cheese balls on serving platter. Skewer them with toothpicks and serve.

# 34 – Strawberries 'n Yogurt

Fresh strawberries and creamy Greek tangerine yogurt combine in this recipe for a stylish but easy to make snack that's even fun to eat.

**Makes** 12 Servings

**Cooking + Prep Time:** 15 minutes

**Ingredients:**

- 12 strawberries, fresh, large
- 1 x 5.3-ounce container of yogurt, Greek tangerine (or flavor of your choice)
- Optional: mini chocolate chips, semi-sweet
- Optional: orange peel, grated

**Instructions:**

1. Wash the strawberries and pat them dry. Scoop out the green tops.

2. Spoon the yogurt into centers of strawberries. Sprinkle with orange peel /or mini chocolate chips, if you like. Serve.

# 35 – Tex Mix

This is quite an easy recipe to make, and it looks very enticing. It's a spicy blend using French fried onions, popcorn and tortilla chips.

**Makes** 18 Servings

**Cooking + Prep Time:** 15 minutes

**Ingredients:**

- 1 individual bag of butter flavored popcorn, microwave
- 4 cups of tortilla chips, crushed lightly

- 2 cans of onions, French fried
- 3 tbsp. of butter, softened
- 1 package of seasoning mix, taco

**Instructions:**

1. Preheat the oven to 350F.

2. Prepare the popcorn using the instructions on the package. Remove any kernels that don't pop. Combine the popped corn with French fried onions and tortilla chips in large sized zipper lock plastic bag.

3. Drizzle melted butter on popcorn mixture. Zip the bag shut and toss, coating the popcorn mixture.

4. Sprinkle the taco seasoning on the mix. Zip the bag shut and toss the mixture again. Spread the mixture on a 10x15" jelly roll pan.

5. Bake for five minutes and stir once about halfway through. Serve.

# Conclusion

This snack cookbook has shown you...

How to use different ingredients to creates many types of snacks, both well-known and rare.

How can you include them in your home recipes?

You can...

- Make small snacks or energy bites by balling together sweet ingredients, for a quick treat that will give you a little energy boost, too.
- Learn to cook with salt and savory ingredients, to make snacks that you can serve at dinner parties or pot luck dinners.
- Enjoy making the delectable chips with everything from apples to sweet potatoes. There are SO many ways to make them great.
- Make snacks using healthy vegetables, for great taste and good nutrition, too.
- Make various types of oh-so-sweet fruit and other sweet snacks that will tempt your family's sweet tooth.

Have fun experimenting! Enjoy the results!